MW01533296

I AM...

A collection of daily affirmations for kids.

Written & Designed by E. Kelley

ISBN: 979-8-9919604-0-3

This book has lived in my heart for a very long
time. I always knew that if one day I was blessed
to be a Mother, I would want my children to know
their worth and believe in themselves.
I dedicate these pages to my daughters,
Cora and Margo.
You are smart, you are beautiful, you are confident,
and you are so very loved.
Today and always.

♥ I AM SMART

♥ I AM BEAUTFUL

♥ I AM CONFIDENT

♥ I AM LOVED

I AM SMART...

From the moment I was born,
my days would be spent
learning and growing
each week as they went.

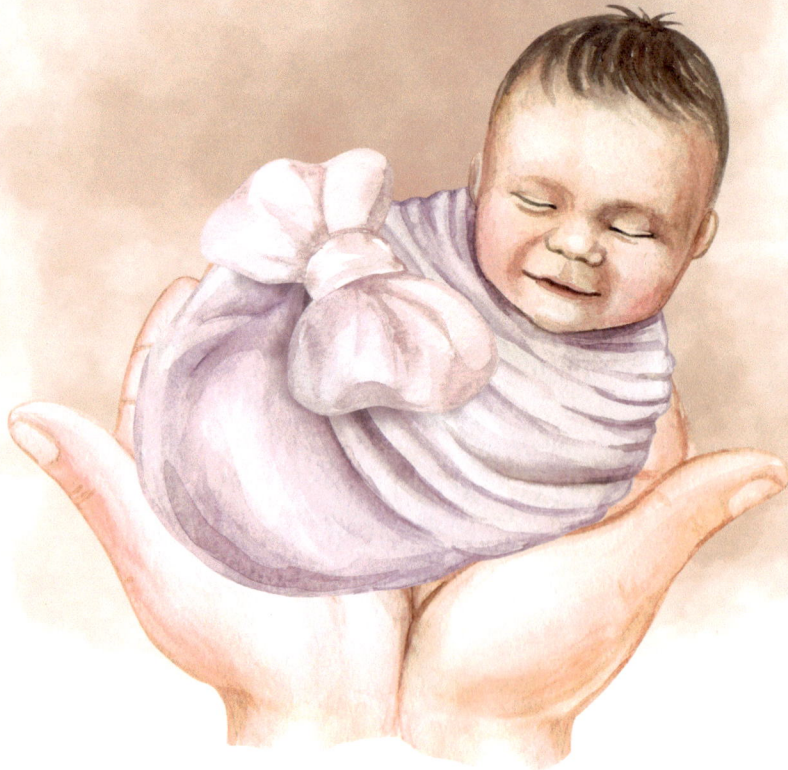

From talking to walking
my mind would get full.
Each day is a new one
at home and at school.

I can learn to read and to write,
to cook and to clean,
to crawl and to climb,
to play and to sing!

There's still so much more
to see and to taste.
I want to keep learning
there's no time to waste!

As I keep growing
and expanding my mind
I never forget
to be humble and kind.

Each day I wake up and remember to say,

"I am smart!
I am smart!
I am smart!
today and always."

I AM BEAUTIFUL...

Beauty is inside and out.
It's what we can see
and what we're about.

My smile, my laugh,
my heart and my mind,
they each have beauty
that's one of a kind.

I am one of a kind!
It's easy to see.
From my head to my toes
there's no one else quite like me!

Each day I wake up and remember to say,

"I am beautiful!
I am beautiful!
I am beautiful!
today and always."

I AM CONFIDENT...

I know I am bold!
I'm bright and I'm true.
I can do anything
I put my mind to.

I am strong, I am smart,
I am capable and kind.
What I wear doesn't matter
as much as my mind.

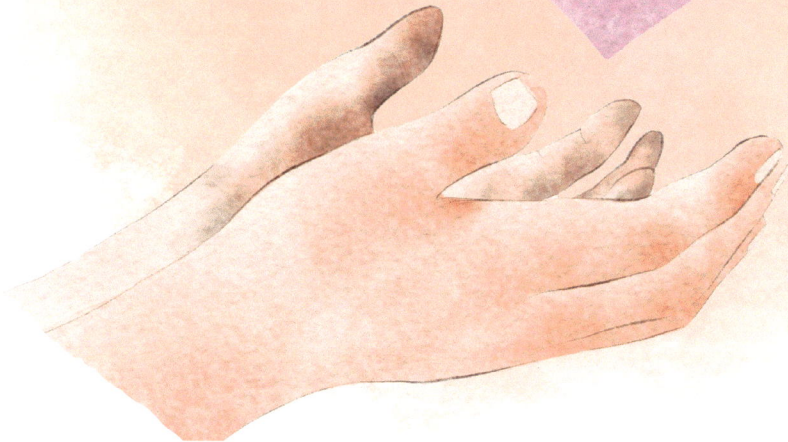

Sometimes I will fail,
it's hard and it's tough.
But I'll just keep trying
and know I'm enough.

Everyday I wake up I remember to say,
"I am confident!
I am confident!
I am confident!
today and always."

I AM LOVED...

I am loved by people
big and small,
near and far,
short and tall.

I am loved by the rain
and the sun and the air!
All gifts from the earth.
All gifts we can share.

I am loved in ways clear to see!
Like when I get hugs and high fives
from people so special to me.

I am loved through nice words
and cheers of support!
Through sharing and caring
and kind acts of all sorts.

Everyday I wake up and remember to say,
"I am loved!
I am loved!
I am loved!
today and always."

In the morning I wake and remember to say,
"Thank you for this beautiful day."
At night when I close my eyes,
I think back on my day and realize,
no matter the good, the funny, or tough.
Each day is a gift, and I know I'm enough.
My worth is not measured by all that's around me.
It's all that I am and all that I can be.
In case I forget, it's easy to find.
I just take a deep breath and make up my mind.
Repeat it again and again if need be
these words are the true definition of me.

I am smart!
I am beautiful!
I am confident!
I am loved!

Made in the USA
Columbia, SC
05 June 2025